YOU CHOOSE
BOOKS

STANLEY HOTEL

A CHILLING INTERACTIVE ADVENTURE

by Allison Lassieur

CAPSTONE PRESS
a capstone imprint

You Choose Books are published by Capstone Press,
1710 Roe Crest Drive, North Mankato, Minnesota 56003
www.mycapstone.com

Library of Congress Cataloging-in-Publication Data
Names: Lassieur, Allison, author.
Title: Stanley Hotel : a chilling interactive adventure / by Allison Lassieur.
Description: North Mankato, Minnesota : Capstone Press, [2017] | Series: You
   choose books. You choose: haunted places | Audience: Ages 8-12. |
   Audience: Grades 4 to 6. | Includes bibliographical references and index.
Identifiers: LCCN 2016035559| ISBN 9781515736509 (library binding) | ISBN
   9781515736554 (ebook pdf)
Subjects: LCSH: Stanley Hotel (Estes Park, Colo.)—Juvenile literature. |
   Haunted hotels—Colorado—Estes Park—Juvenile literature. | CYAC: Haunted
   places—Colorado—Estes Park.
Classification: LCC BF1474.5 .L37 2017 | DDC 133.1/29788/68--dc23
LC record available at https://lccn.loc.gov/2016035559

Editorial Credits
Mari Bolte, editor; Heidi Thompson, designer; Wanda Winch, media researcher;
Gene Bentdahl, production specialist

Photo Credits
Alamy: Blaine Harrington III, 103, Ed Endicott, 73, LatitudeStock/Stuart Cox, 49;
Courtesy of David Sanden, 17, 86; Courtesy of Joy Yehle, 38; Courtesy of Long Island
Paranormal Investigators, 98; Courtesy of the Stanley Hotel, 4, 10, 14, 21, 28, 32,
42, 71, 100, Zach Connor, cover; Getty Images: Blaine Harrington III, 53; Henry
Yau, 66-67; iStockphoto: William Howell, 75; Louise Hung, 24, 93; Nefer Khepri,
PhD.,104; Shutterstock: Darla Hallmark, 60, happykanppy, background design, Igor
Vitkovskiy, fog element, Natata, cover (sign), 1 (sign), Plateresca, paper design, run4it, ink
painting background, saki80, frame design, STILLFX, grey grunge texture; Thinkstock:
RiverNorthPhotography, 6

Printed in Canada.
10050S17

TABLE OF CONTENTS

INTRODUCTION

YOU are trapped in a haunted hotel on a family vacation gone awry. What was meant to be a fun ski getaway in the Rocky Mountains has become a night of terror at the Stanley Hotel. A blizzard shrieks outside, and inside there are ghosts around every corner. It's late, and the few guests who are also trapped with you in the hotel have gone to bed. The living ones, that is. Are you brave enough to investigate who—or what—else might have checked in?

The first settlers arrived in Estes Park in the 1860s. Tourists began vacationing there near the end of the century. The Stanley Hotel opened in 1909.

CHECK IN

"That's it? That's the most haunted hotel in America?" Your brother Alex snorts into his drink cup beside you in the back seat as the famous Stanley Hotel comes into view. "It doesn't look so haunted."

"Just you wait," your dad says from the front seat, in his creepiest horror-movie voice. But you agree with Alex. As the car turns onto the road leading to the hotel, disappointment washes over you. All you can see are glimpses of a huge building with a blood-red roof peeking out among the trees. The Rocky Mountains rise majestically behind the hotel. Above the mountains, the sky is filled with ominous dark clouds. It's pretty, but not scary or spooky like you expected.

Turn the page.

Your mom taps on her phone, frowning. "The weather report doesn't look good," she says for the hundredth time since you got on the road this morning. "They're saying it's the worst freak snowstorm in years."

"At least we made it to the hotel in time," your dad says, as he pulls up to the front. "I'm sure it'll blow over tonight and we can go skiing tomorrow, just like we planned."

For weeks your family has been planning this ski trip to Colorado. The only place your mom wanted to stay was the Stanley Hotel in Estes Park. The Stanley, more than a hundred years old, had all the antique old elegance that you and your mom like. When you found out about the Stanley's ghostly reputation, things got even more interesting. How cool would it be to stay at a real haunted hotel?

You expected a dark, foreboding Victorian building with hanging shutters and creaking steps. But instead, the stark white hotel sits grandly on the snow-covered ground. The dark clouds help with the ghostly mood, but you're feeling let down.

Everyone spills out of the car as the hotel staff helps unload the luggage and ski gear. You grab your suitcase and casually look up, noticing the rows of windows down the front of the old hotel.

Your eyes stop on one window. A shadowy figure stands in the frame. It is hazy, like a blurry picture. You can't make out its face, but somehow you know it's staring right at you. A cold wind blows across your face as the sun goes behind a storm cloud. You blink. When you look back, the figure is gone.

Turn the page.

The Stanley Hotel has 140 guest rooms available year-round. Many guests have reported seeing someone looking out the window of room 407.

"Did you see that?" you say, pointing to the window. Alex throws his skis over his shoulder and gives you a shove.

"Not going to work," he says, grinning. "No such things as ghosts. It's just a way for this old hotel to make money."

But you know you saw something.

Shaken, you enter the lobby and cross gleaming hardwood floors, walking past comfortable furniture to the marble and wood front desk. It's quiet. *Too* quiet. The lobby is empty except for your family. Now that you think about it, the parking lot was empty too.

"Where is everyone?" you ask the desk clerk, trying not to sound worried.

"It's the storm," the woman replies. "We've been getting cancellations all day." As if on cue, dark clouds pass overhead, dimming the lobby. Alex's eyes widen, and then he shakes it off and laughs.

"Don't worry," the clerk says, seeing your faces. "You'll be safe here. There are a few other guests so you won't be alone." Then she leans forward conspiratorially and whispers, "Then again, you're never REALLY alone at the Stanley Hotel."

Turn the page.

Alex laughs, and the clerk winks. "That's true whether there are living guests here or not," she adds.

Your mom puts her phone away, not hearing what the woman said or seeing your nervous reaction. "What rooms are available?" she asks.

The woman smiles. "You're very lucky! Two of our most haunted rooms are available. Would you like room 217, or 418?"

"*Most* haunted?" you ask. "Like ... just how haunted are we talking?"

The woman smiles again. "Wait and see."

To stay in room 217, go to page 13.

To stay in room 418, turn to page 44.

You flip a coin and choose room 217. The carpeted halls are eerily quiet as you walk toward your room. The hallway stretches long and empty behind you. Yet you feel as though someone is watching you.

"What's so special about 217, I wonder," you say aloud in a hushed voice.

"You've never heard of room 217?" the bellhop says as he pushes the cart of luggage. "You have heard of the writer Stephen King, right?"

You nod. Your mom and dad read his horror stories, and you've seen a few movies on cable that were based on them. "So what does he have to do with anything?"

"Stephen King and his wife Tabitha stayed for one night," the bellhop says. "They were here the very last night the hotel was open that year, and they were the only guests."

Turn the page.

The circular staircase starts on the second floor. So many ghosts have been seen here that it is also known as "The Vortex."

The bellhop gives you sidelong glance. "After a single night in that room," he intones slowly, "King got the idea for his book, *The Shining*. It's about a haunted hotel. The ghosts there drive a man insane."

"Ahhh!" Alex suddenly shoves you from behind and you let out a screech. He laughs, happy that he got you.

You glare at Alex, but your heart is beating fast. You've never seen the movie but you've heard it's one of the scariest films ever made.

The bellhop seems to read your mind. "If you've never seen it, don't worry," he says. "One of the channels on the TV in your room plays it on a loop."

A short hallway dead-ends into a wooden door, with another door beside it. "Here it is, room 217," the bellhop says.

"You two can have that room," your dad says. "We'll take the one next door. Get changed and meet us downstairs for dinner."

Slowly you open the door, heart beating furiously. You're not sure what to expect, but it's just an ordinary room. There are two large antique beds, some furniture, and a wooden table with two chairs. Outside, the wind has picked up, moaning mournfully as it rattles the windows. Even though it's early, the storm clouds have made it almost fully dark outside.

Turn the page.

15

"So, um, what's in this room, anyway?" you ask the bellhop, who is standing in the doorway.

The bellhop glances into the room. You notice he has pushed the bags into the room without ever crossing the door's threshold. "There are noises," he says in a low voice. "Things moving around on their own. Doors opening and closing by themselves."

Without another word he hurries off. To ease your mind, you open all the doors and turn on all the lights. Alex is sprawled on the bed flipping channels on the television. He finds the one dedicated to *The Shining* and, grinning at you, leaves it there.

"I'm starving," he says. "Let's go find Mom and Dad downstairs."

"I'm not really hungry," you reply, your stomach suddenly in knots.

Alex jumps up and heads for the door. "Do what you want," he says.

To stay in the room, turn to page 18.

To meet your family in the restaurant, turn to page 32.

Mystery surrounds the hotel's second floor.

The door shuts behind Alex with a soft click and you're all alone in the room. The first thing you do is turn off the TV and lie down. You can hear the howl of the storm and the icy hiss of hard-driven snow against the windows. You still feel as though you're being watched, but you know deep down there's no one here. The soft bed feels great after sitting in the car all afternoon. Soon you're snoring softly.

A loud crash, followed by a slamming noise, wakes you. You sit upright, your heart beating. The room is pitch black. The only light is the red dot from the smoke alarm high on the wall. The howling of the wind fills the room. *The storm must be right over the hotel,* you think.

The presence you felt earlier is still there. Sitting there, alone in the dark, the hairs on the back of your neck prickle and rise.

"Alex? Mom? Dad?" Your voice is barely above a whisper. No one answers, and the darkness seems to close in even more.

You stumble through the room with your hands stretched into the darkness. You try to convince yourself that you're alone, that you won't touch anything ... unexpected. Still, your hands don't linger any longer than they need to.

This is crazy! There's no one here, you think angrily to yourself. The electricity has gone off because of the storm, that's all. Your family is probably together in the dining room, waiting it out.

Suddenly an idea pops into your head. Your phone! You grope in your pocket. It's not there. Where did you leave it?

Turn the page.

As you make your way toward the bed, your shoe connects with something hard. Reluctantly, you nudge it with your foot and realize you've found a glass. As you feel with your hands, you realize it's cracked in half.

Where did it come from? Then you remember the loud crash that woke you. The only glass items in the room were the drinking glasses in the bathroom beside the ice bucket. How did it get out here? Was someone—or something—in the room with you while you slept?

And then you remember: The bathroom is where you left your phone.

To get your phone, go to page 21.

To leave the room, turn to page 25.

As you turn toward the bathroom, a roar fills your ears. Your feet seem to move on their own as you stumble around the room. Waving your hands wildly in front of you for balance, you slam your knuckles against the closed bathroom door. Closed? You opened it before you fell asleep! Then you remember the slam that woke you. You push the door open and step inside.

Some employees at the hotel refuse to go into the bathroom in room 217.

Turn the page.

Your fingers slide along the edge of the sink until you find your phone. At your touch, the phone lights up the room in a dim glow. A drinking glass—or what's left of it—is on the counter. It's cracked, with large chunks broken off, but it's sitting upright next to the sink, as though someone placed it there.

You jump as water suddenly shoots out of the sink's faucet.

You don't even bother to look for the room key as you run to the door, the light from your phone guiding the way.

There's no answer when you pound on the door to your parents' room. They must still be downstairs. You glance at your phone and gasp. It's after 1 a.m.! Where could they be?

You can hear the storm, even from inside the hallway. But somewhere in the darkness, beyond the thin light of your phone, you hear voices too.

"Mom? Dad?" you yell, sprinting down the hallway.

You run down the hall, but the voices fade into the shrieking storm. Suddenly your phone goes into sleep mode. The darkness closes in, and you begin to panic. You tap your phone back to life, but the "low battery" light comes on.

You dial your mom's number, but the call goes straight to voicemail. The same with Alex's phone. A fresh wave of fear washes over you. You can't get back into your room, even if you wanted to. Your only choice is to check the hotel's lobby.

Turn the page.

The famous elevator was installed in 1909. It was updated from hydraulics to electric in 1935.

You reach the elevator and press the button.

Nothing happens.

To use the emergency stairwell, turn to page 55.

To go to the lobby through the main hallway, turn to page 58.

The phone isn't worth it, you think as you slam the door to your room behind you.

You press against the wall in the darkness, your heart thumping. The walls of the hotel vibrate with the power of the storm outside. You pound on your parents' door, but there's no answer.

Far down the hallway, a dim light catches your eye. It seems to float in the darkness, darting here and there.

To go toward the light, turn to page 26.

To stay where you are, turn to page 62.

You walk cautiously toward the moving light.

"Who's there?" a voice calls. The light stops, trembling, in the darkness.

"I'm a guest," you reply, your voice trembling. " ... Uh, a live one."

Laughter floats down the hall. "That's good to hear." The light moves toward you quickly. Your rescuer is a man in a hotel uniform. Your knees almost buckle from the relief.

"Did you get locked out too? The electronic key system went down with the electricity." He frowns. "It's not supposed to do that."

You nod, still too jumpy to speak. He gives you an understanding look. "Not the best place to be lost in the dark, is it?" he asks. "Come on."

You follow him down the hotel's main staircase. Halfway down, you get the feeling that you're being watched again. You stop and look around. Your guide keeps going, disappearing into the restaurant. Once again you're alone in the dark. Then you hear the low hum of voices from another direction.

To follow your guide into the restaurant, turn to page 28.

To go toward the voices, turn to page 30.

"Wait!" you yell, but he's gone. You rush to catch up. But when you enter the dining room, there's nobody there. The large room is empty. Shining tables and chairs line the floor. You can see the blue-glow of the blizzard through the windows. The storm your mom was tracking is in full force. A huge mirrored bar stretches along one wall. It reminds you of a saloon from an old western.

The Whiskey Bar & Lounge at the Cascades Restaurant leads to a covered patio with a waterfall and sculpture garden.

You take a step toward the bar. Suddenly a chair slides into your path, and you crash painfully to the floor. You climb to your feet, hip aching and palms sore. The chair that you're sure attacked you has returned to its place at the table.

Dizzy with fear and limping in pain, you make your way to the kitchen. The sound of clinking glass is coming from the back. You step toward the noise. With each step you take, the air gets colder. Soon it feels as though you're walking in a freezer.

To keep moving toward the sound, turn to page 64.

To try to escape the restaurant, turn to page 66.

An uneasy feeling fills you as you move toward the voices. They're coming from behind a set of large wooden doors on one end of the lobby. You see light streaming from the crack between the doors, and hear music and laughter. You hear the clatter of tableware and china. Is it a party? Maybe your parents are here!

Relieved, you open the door. The bright lights are blinding after the darkness of the hotel. This is the MacGregor room, the grand ballroom of the Stanley Hotel. You step inside and close the door, scanning the crowd for your family. The people are dressed in old-fashioned clothing, with elegant long skirts and tuxedos. Couples waltz to the music from the old piano. Maids in frilly uniforms move through the crowd. Viewing the scene makes you uneasy. You can't imagine your parents here. Dad, in a tuxedo? No way. Your skin starts to prickle.

As you watch, the partygoers seem to drift in and out, becoming faded versions of themselves before phasing back to a more solid form. This can't be happening. The music plays on, but it sounds far away, as if you're hearing it over a great distance. Swirls of icy cold air pass over you. Is this for real? Or is your imagination going crazy?

To leave the ballroom, turn to page 69.

To stay, turn to page 72.

You get an uneasy feeling as the family is seated for dinner in the Cascades Restaurant at the hotel. The coming storm creates a weird greenish glow as the wind rises, moaning against the windows. As you glance at the menu, you suddenly notice that your family is alone in the restaurant. The waiter appears and takes your order, then disappears again. The only other person in the room is the bartender.

The hotel can be rented out for weddings, meetings, haunted tours, and psychic consultations.

"Come on," Alex says. "Let's go order at the bar!" He drags you out of your seat. The huge, gleaming wood bar looks like something out of an old movie, with tall mirrors on the wall behind it. Reluctantly you follow Alex, where he orders a Coke in his best Western drawl.

The drinks arrive and you nervously sit at the bar, half-listening as Alex raves about the ski slopes. A small movement catches your eye, and you flinch back. Alex's glass is sliding silently across the bar. It stops an inch from your hand.

"Hey, that's mine," Alex says, grabbing the glass. You blink, not sure you really saw what you think you saw. *No more caffeine for me*, you think, pushing your own glass away and returning to the table.

Turn the page.

During the entire meal, no one else comes into the restaurant. By the time you've finished, you're jumpy, and your stomach is in knots. The wind blows against the windows, icy snow hissing against the glass. The lights flicker once, then twice. Even the bartender is gone now.

"We're going back to the room," your dad says. "It's been a long day."

"Let's do some exploring," Alex says, jumping up. "Maybe we'll see some ghosts!"

To go back to the room, go to page 35.

To explore the hotel, turn to page 39.

You don't want to explore. Alex calls you a name and stomps off. You want to tell him not to go, but he's gone before you work up the nerve.

Your unease grows as you walk through the empty hotel. At every turn you expect to see some signs of life, but no one appears. Your parents feel it too. Your mom trembles as she gives you an extra-long hug goodnight.

When you open the door to your room, there are noises coming from the bathroom. Someone is running water. Could Alex be back already? Nervously, you creep toward the closed door and listen for familiar sounds. But all you can hear is water. Wiping your sweaty hands on your jeans, you reach for the knob and open the door.

Turn the page.

The shower is going full blast, and foggy steam swirls in the air. You grab the shower curtain, pulling so hard it rips off the metal rings. But no one is there.

Alex, you jerk, you think, trying to laugh about it. Turning off the shower, you flop on the bed. You're going to get him back. But you can't shake the strange feeling in the pit of your stomach.

You flip through the television's channels, trying to keep your mind occupied. You can't stop feeling as though something is wrong, though. You turn down the volume as you think.

Then you notice all the suitcases stacked neatly in one corner of the room. You didn't do that. You get off the bed and pull open one of the dresser drawers. Your clothing is folded neatly inside.

You pick up the phone and press a button. "Hello, front desk," a friendly voice says. "How can I help you?"

"Hi," you say. "I'm in room 217. Has housekeeping or maintenance or someone else been in our room since we arrived?"

There is a pause at the other end. "I'm sorry," the voice says. "You said 217?"

"Yes." You break out in a cold sweat. "Why?"

"No one on the staff has been in your room today," the voice says. Then there's a click as the call disconnects.

You put down the receiver and stare at the stacked luggage. There has to be an explanation. One of your parents must have put everything away. That's it. It must be.

Turn the page.

Room 217 is also known as the Stephen King Suite.

Taking a deep breath, you relax. Folded clothes aren't scary! You've got the room to yourself until Alex gets back, and you're wasting it worrying about nothing.

Then the hotel trembles and the lights flicker again. Maybe being alone isn't such a good idea.

To go look for Alex, turn to page 41.

To stay in the room, turn to page 74.

The storm outside hits the hotel with full force, blasting icy snow against the windows like shotgun pellets. Despite the desk clerk's assurance that there are other guests, the lobby is empty and eerie.

You stand near a large table as Alex peruses a brochure about the hotel. The table holds an enormous bouquet of flowers in a crystal vase. As you watch, one of the flower stems bends all by itself. The petals ripple slightly, as though someone is smelling the flower. Then the stem bounces back into place, quivering slightly.

Heart hammering, you ask, "Did ... did you see that?"

"See what?" Alex is folding up the pamphlet and heading toward one of the large meeting rooms. "Come on, this way."

Turn the page.

"I don't think I want to do this," you say, uneasy at the idea of exploring the empty—and possibly haunted—hallways.

"Fine, be a wimp," Alex says, waving toward the elevator. "I'm going ghost hunting."

To take the stairs back to your room, turn to page 83.

To take the elevator, turn to page 85.

You step out of the room, closing the door firmly behind you. You head straight for the stairs. When you hear footsteps, you stop, grateful that you're not alone. But the hallway is empty. *The quicker I find Alex, the better,* you think. You send your brother a text while keeping an uneasy eye on the empty hallway.

You jump as your phone chirps.

I'm in the lobby. —Alex

Anxious to find your brother, you descend the main staircase two steps at a time. To your surprise, a woman is coming up the stairs. She is dressed in an elegant hat and gown. Her dress is long, and she holds up the hem to avoid stepping on it. You wonder if there's some kind of costume party in the hotel tonight. Your blood runs cold as she passes you. You can see through her.

Guests have reported passing ghosts going up and down the grand staircase.

You press yourself against the railing as she passes. A cold, rose-scented draft seems to come off her body, making goosebumps rise on your arms. You can't tear your eyes away from her, but she passes you as if you're not there. When she reaches the top of the steps, she disappears.

Your heart is pounding, and you can't move. It takes a few minutes to calm down and breathe normally. Holding the railing, you make your way slowly down the stairs. When you reach the lobby, Alex is nowhere to be seen. The lobby is to the right. The Billiard Room is to the left.

To stop at the reception desk, turn to page 78.

To go to the Billiard Room, turn to page 80.

"Room 418's on the most haunted floor," the clerk says as she hands you your room keys.

Alex grins, but your stomach flutters. "Will we see ghosts up there?" you ask hesitantly.

"Likely," the clerk replies seriously. "The fourth floor has more reports of paranormal activity than any other. Back in the day, it was where the nannies and children stayed."

She leans in and whispers, "And room 418 is the most haunted room in the whole hotel."

You're completely creeped out, but Alex laughs. "Baby ghosts! Oooohhhh!" he says, wiggling his fingers at you. Your parents are too busy with the luggage and ski equipment to notice your obnoxious brother. Sighing, you grab some gear and head for the elevator. Maybe Alex is right—maybe the "ghosts" are just a story to attract tourists.

You all squeeze into the elevator. The polished wood and brass on the century-old elevator still glow. The car rattles gently as it moves upward.

When you reach the third floor, the doors open unexpectedly. You look out in time to see a little girl with a head of curls running down the hallway. Childlike laughter echoes after her.

"Just some kid pressing buttons," you mutter as the elevator door closes and takes you to your floor. As you gather outside your room, you hear what sounds like two men arguing.

"Is someone already in this room?" your dad wonders. He swipes his key card and pushes open the door. Instantly the voices stop.

"Must have been another room," your mom says. There's no one here, but the air is icy cold. You shiver, but it has nothing to do with the temperature.

Turn the page.

"Someone must have put the air conditioning on instead of the heat," your dad says. He checks the thermostat and a strange expression crosses his face.

"Weird," he says. "The heat is on."

"And the hotel doesn't have air conditioning," your mom points out.

"I'm sure it's the ghosts playing tricks on us," Alex says, flopping on the bed. "Hurry and unpack. I want to go to the gift shop."

"Dad and I are going to go look for some ghosts," Mom says, reading a brochure. "You can join us if you want."

To go ghost hunting with your parents, go to page 47.

To go to the gift shop with Alex, turn to page 88.

As you stand at the door waiting for your parents to get ready, you hear a crash from outside. It sounds like a herd of kids are running up and down the hallway. Their footsteps tread noisily on the carpet. *Someone must have a ball,* you think, as muted thudding noises cause the walls to shake.

When you leave the room, the children are gone. The sound of their laughter rings out from behind several room doors. "I'm going to say something to management about this," your mom says, irritated.

At the reception desk downstairs the clerk listens to your mom's complaints.

"Let me ... get my manager," she stammers. "One moment, please." She disappears in the back, and you have to wait several minutes before she and the manager appear.

Turn the page.

"I understand your issue, ma'am," the manager says. "Unfortunately, there's a problem. We don't actually have any families with small children checked into the hotel today."

"That's not possible," your mom replies, a nervous edge in her voice. "We heard them."

"I saw a little girl running down the third floor hallway," you add.

The mansger nods. "That happens a lot on the upper floors," he says. "That's where the children used to stay when they visited with their parents."

Your mom's face turns white and her hands grip the counter. You're sure you don't look much better. That curly-haired girl looked so real. Are they really saying she was a ghost?

"Th-thank you," your mom says, slowly backing away from the desk.

"I'm through with ghost hunting for now," your mom stammers as your dad and Alex appear. "I'm going to dinner—and your father is coming with me." Your dad shoots her a surprised look, then shrugs. They head toward the restaurant.

"Hey, did you just say you saw a ghost on the third floor?" Two guys and a girl in their mid-twenties approach the front desk. They are loaded down with cameras and other equipment.

Curious guests can take one of the hotel's ghost walks, history tours, or meet with the hotel's resident psychic. Ghost hunters are also invited to spend the night.

Turn the page.

"Um, why?" you reply.

"We're ghost hunters," the girl says proudly, brushing snow out of her hair. "I'm Amy, and this is Mike and Josh. We're here to get evidence of the Stanley Hotel's paranormal activity."

"We'll tell you everything we know if we can stay and watch," Alex says, thinking fast. The trio looks at each other, then nods.

"Okay," Josh says. "We're going to check out the downstairs areas first. The Pinon Room and Music Room report a lot of activity."

To peek into the Pinon Room, go to page 51.

To go to the Music Room, turn to page 90.

"This used to be called the Smoking Room," Mike says, entering the Pinon Room. You hang back, suddenly ill at ease. You don't want to be in this room, and you have the disturbing feeling that something else doesn't want you there, either. Your apprehension rises as you pass over the room's threshold. Nobody else seems to notice anything, though, and you don't want to look like a coward.

There's a fireplace on one side of the room and an ornate, mirrored cabinet on the opposite wall. The cabinet makes your senses tingle even more, and you move to the opposite end of the room.

Suddenly the room is filled with the smell of pipe smoke. Everyone starts coughing and choking. You think you might be sick. Then the smell disappears as fast as it came.

Turn the page.

"What was that?" Josh gasps.

You're done ignoring the signs. It's time to leave.

"I'll meet you outside," you say. You push the door to exit—but it pushes back! Then it swings hard into your face, as though someone has shoved it. There's a crack as the edge of the door connects with your forehead, sending you flying to the floor.

"Are you OK?" Alex asks, helping you up.

"I've got to get out of here," you croak. Alex pushes the door open, straining to hold it as you dash through. As he lets go to exit himself, the door swings violently, barely missing him.

You collapse in a lobby chair. Alex, for once, doesn't have a know-it-all response to what just happened.

The lobby has been restored to its early-20th-century furnishings.

The ghost hunters stagger out of the Pinon Room, joining you in the lobby.

"That was just incredible," Josh says, his voice unsteady.

"Readings through the roof!" Amy says, checking the equipment. "I can't believe we got such a strong signal right away!"

Turn the page.

"Where to next?" Mike asks. "I hear there's a secret tunnel under the hotel."

"There's a lot of weird things that happen on the fourth floor," Alex suggests helpfully. You shoot him a dirty look. But he's not wrong. And you're with professionals now.

To check out the tunnel, turn to page 93.

To go back to the fourth floor, turn to page 97.

The emergency stairs seem like a safe choice. That is, until you step into the dark, narrow stairwell. It's just one floor, you repeat over and over to yourself. Clutching the rail with one hand and your lighted phone in the other, you head down. The voices get louder as you descend into the darkness. Thankfully, you reach the door to the lobby. You expect to see people and lights, an explanation for the voices you hear. Instead, the short hallway is as dark as the rest of the hotel.

Tentatively, you take a step forward. Then you feel something cold brush past you in the dark. Something ice-cold grips your wrist.

"Leave me alone! Let go!" you shout. As you struggle, you drop your phone. The light lingers for a short second before turning off. You're left alone in the dark.

Turn the page.

You hear the sound of footsteps on carpet.
They're coming toward you. Unable to move,
all you can do is shrink back.

A bright light momentarily blinds you.
"Hey, what are you doing here?" It's Alex.
The light is from his phone. "I heard you yell.
What happened?"

Alex's warm hands on your shoulders replace
the ghostlike icy grip on your wrists. You don't
know whether to laugh or cry with relief. He
takes you to the lobby, which is filled with people
and hotel staff. A generator powers this area,
filling it with bright, safe light. You run to your
mom's outstretched arms.

"Whoa, are you OK?" she asks, worried.
"When the electricity went off we couldn't get
back into our rooms, so the hotel staff set us up
down here. I thought you'd be asleep all night."

You tell them everything. Alex looks at you with a strange expression and you brace for more teasing. Instead, he points to your arm.

"Look," he says in an odd voice. You couldn't see them in the dark, but now in this light room it's clear. Several thin, red marks encircle your wrist. Your eyes meet. "Wow," he whistles softly. "No way." He doesn't say another word as you all wrap up in blankets and try to get some sleep on the lobby floor.

By morning the storm has passed. You wake up to sunlight streaming through the lobby windows. The marks on your wrists are gone. Without a word, your dad goes to the front desk to change rooms—and floors—as the rest of your family heads to breakfast. What a way to start a vacation!

THE END

To follow another path, turn to page 12.
To learn more about the Stanley Hotel, turn to page 101.

By the time you get near the main staircase, you're drenched in sweat. You notice with a start that the hallway is no longer completely dark. There's a ghostly blue light that lingers near the open doorway at the top of the stairs.

You turn off your phone and slowly approach the light. It seems to get brighter the closer you get. You also begin to hear voices.

Carefully you peek around the corner. The top of the main staircase is lined with huge windows. The white snowstorm outside reflecting off the window is the thing causing the blue light. Mirrors on the wall enhance the effect. And the voices, you are relieved to see, is a group of people moving around in the lobby below.

You nearly cry with relief. The hotel's not haunted—it's all been your imagination!

You start flying down the stairs, taking them two at a time. You're about halfway down when something hits you in the shins, hard. You cry out as you lose your balance, crashing down the hard wooden steps.

"Honey, are you OK?" your mom cries, helping you up. Your dad and Alex are right behind her. "What happened?"

You take one final look back up the staircase. There's nothing there.

Shaken, you tell them everything that happened since you woke up. Your parents exchange worried glances. "When the electricity went out we couldn't get back into our rooms," she says. "I figured you'd sleep through the storm. I'm sorry you got so scared in the dark."

"It wasn't just the dark! Someone tripped me on the stairs," you insist. "Look."

Turn the page.

Your dad shines a light as you pull up your pants leg. There's an angry red mark on your skin just above your ankle.

A hotel employee overhears you and comes over to check out the mark. She nods. "Yup, that's one of the kids."

"Kids?" you ask. "There wasn't anyone on the stairs with me."

Elizabeth, Lucy, Eddie, and Paul are four ghosts often seen and heard in the hotel.

"Several guests have reported being kicked or pushed on the main staircase lately, when no one else is with them," she explains. "We think it's one of the ghost children who live here. They like to play tricks."

You stare back up the staircase. You almost think you see a humanlike shape in the eerie blue hue—but no, that has to be your imagination. The next day dawns bright and sunny, but your family has had enough. You check out and head straight home, leaving the haunted Stanley Hotel behind forever.

THE END

To follow another path, turn to page 12.
To learn more about the Stanley Hotel, turn to page 101.

You sink to the floor, trying to be as small and silent as you can. Whatever that is, you don't want it to find you. The light continues to move up and down the hallway but it doesn't get any closer. Finally it fades away and you're alone in the inky darkness.

Suddenly, out of the darkness, a shadowy gray figure appears. It's a woman dressed in an old-fashioned maid's dress. She wears a white cap. The air around her radiates cold. An icy breeze passes over you as she comes near. The ghost pauses at the door to your room, then walks through it with a soft "pop."

Your head spins. *I think I'm going to be sick* is the last thought you have before passing out. The next thing you know, Alex is shaking you awake.

"What are you doing out here asleep?" your mom asks. Your head aches, but you tell them what you remember. You can tell Alex and your dad are skeptical. Alex swipes the key card and goes into room 217. You hear a muffled cry. A minute later he reappears, face white.

He refuses to say what he saw, but he won't go back into the room, either. Your parents pack up, and the family heads home. You have nightmares for months afterward, filled with a screaming white snowstorm and chilling ghostly faces.

THE END

To follow another path, turn to page 12.
To learn more about the Stanley Hotel, turn to page 101.

You have to find your missing guide. You wrap your arms around yourself for warmth and keep going.

The tinkling sound of glasses is louder as you approach the kitchen. You hurry toward the sounds as fast as you can.

"Why did you leave me?" you demand as you turn the corner into the beverage area. "Hello?" There's nothing here but stacks of glasses.

"Where are you!?" you scream. You move to leave the kitchen. As soon as you turn your back, the sound of clinking glass starts again. You freeze, but are too afraid to look back. Something sharp strikes you in the temple, hard enough to knock you off your feet. The last thing you remember is an empty crystal glass rolling on the floor next to your head.

You wake up in a bright hospital room. It's daylight and your family surrounds your bed.

"What happened?" you whisper. Your head is covered with bandages.

"The hotel staff found you in the kitchen after the storm," your dad said. "You must have fainted, and hit your head as you fell."

"There's a crazy-looking bruise on your leg too," Alex says. "Did you get into a fight with a ghost?" He laughs at his own joke.

You close your eyes and shake your head. "You wouldn't believe me if I told you," you say.

THE END

To follow another path, turn to page 12.
To learn more about the Stanley Hotel, turn to page 101.

You make it back into the lobby. When you got here this afternoon it felt alive and inviting. Now, a sense of foreboding hangs in the air. The darkness is spooky, and the weird blue hue coming in the windows doesn't help the atmosphere.

A movement near the reception desk catches your eye. Someone is there! You almost laugh with relief as you stagger to the desk. It's a woman, and she smiles kindly at you.

"Where is everyone?" you sputter, gripping the edge of the desk. "I need to find my family."

The woman continues smiling at you. Annoyed, you look for a name tag or other identifying feature. Then you realize that she's wearing an old-fashioned dress with a lace collar. And ... she's glowing. She looks down at her hands, and fades away.

In 2016 a guest took a panoramic picture of the lobby with his cell phone. A ghost—or pair of ghosts—was spotted at the top of the stairs.

Turn the page.

"No," you whisper. "No!" Your foot catches on something as you back away from the desk. You fall, hitting your head on a heavy table. Before you lose consciousness, the woman appears over you, her eerie smile the last thing you see before you close your eyes. The next time you open them you find your body is made of mist. You've joined the spirits at the Stanley Hotel, and it looks like you'll never be checking out.

THE END

To follow another path, turn to page 12.
To learn more about the Stanley Hotel, turn to page 101.

Terrified, you slowly back up, afraid to take your eyes off the party going on in front of you. You find the doors and quickly slide out, shutting them quietly. It's not quiet enough though—the door makes a faint click. At the sound, the light disappears from beneath the door and the room goes instantly silent. You lean on the door, breathing heavily, afraid to move.

"There you are!"

You spin around at the sound, ready to run. The hotel worker shines his flashlight in your face, blinding you.

"Sorry I lost you," he says. "Hey, are you OK? Why are you standing out here in the dark? Everyone is in the ballroom. You can just go in."

"No, no," you whisper, your hands shaking. "Not going in there again."

Turn the page.

The man doesn't hear you. Reaching past you, he pulls open the heavy door. You yell and jump back. He gives you a strange look and strides into the room. Breathing hard, you peer inside.

The old-fashioned party guests are gone. Several small groups of people—wearing jeans and T-shirts—are standing around or sitting at tables. A few emergency lanterns cast a dim light in the darkened room.

"Are you OK?" your mom asks, hugging you.

You stare at her and slowly shake your head. "How long have you been here?" you croak.

"Since the lights went out, right after dinner," Alex says, giving you a strange look. "Man, you look like you've seen a ghost!"

You sink into a chair and don't move or speak until morning. Not even Alex can change your mood. When the storm is over your dad checks out and you climb into the car, not looking back. You never tell anyone what happened in the ballroom. But your dreams are filled with music and dancing, and every night for months you wake up screaming.

THE END

To follow another path, turn to page 12.
To learn more about the Stanley Hotel, turn to page 101.

The hotel opened on June 22, 1909. Rooms ranged in price from $5 to $8 per night.

Slowly, reluctantly, you walk through the ballroom. You really don't want to be there, but it feels as if something is pulling you forward.

None of the dancers notice you. Even when the crowds press closer, you don't get a second glance. You notice when they touch you, though—a cold shiver runs up your spine every time you make contact.

A cold shock runs up your arm—a spirit has taken your hand in its own. You feel a tug as the spirit begins to dance and you have no choice but to follow.

You spin and twirl, unable to pull away from the chilling grasp. The music grows louder and faster. You become dizzy. The ghost's cold arms crush you, squeezing your heart until you collapse. "Thank you," she whispers softly into your ear. Then you lose consciousness.

No one ever finds your body. But many workers and visitors at the hotel witness the ghostly parties in the MacGregor room. They describe vintage décor, smiling dancers, eerie music—and a ghost that looks uncannily similar to a guest who went missing years before.

THE END

To follow another path, turn to page 12.
To learn more about the Stanley Hotel, turn to page 101.

The piano was a gift to Flora Stanley on the hotel's opening day. Rumors say both the Stanleys still like to play.

You shake off your uneasiness and flop back down on the bed, turning on the TV and flipping channels while trying to ignore the storm outside. There's nothing good on, and the moaning wind makes you edgy. Nervous, you get up and pace the room. Movement catches your eye—one of the pillows sitting in the middle of the bed slides to the floor.

You stare dumbly at the pillow. There was no way it could have just fallen off on its own. You're still trying to figure things out when your phone rings, scaring you so badly that you jump halfway across the room. Your hands shake as you pull out your phone. It's a text from your friend Jordan. *Seen any ghosts yet? Haha!*

Not yet, you type back.

You're both irritated with your friend's timing and glad for the human contact. With your arm outstretched, you make a goofy face and snap a selfie. *Just another boring night,* you type before hitting send.

Instantly your phone pings again. The four words on your screen make your heart freeze.

Who's that with you?

Rooms 217 and 401 aren't the only rooms with lots of paranormal activity. Rooms 407, 428, and 1302 are also said to be haunted.

Turn the page.

You scroll up your messages and enlarge the photo you took. There's your face. But there's something behind you too. A shadowy figure sits on the bed behind you, its arm outstretched. You drop the phone. You can't turn around. You want to move, to run, but your body is paralyzed with fear. *Get to the door,* you think. *Just get to the door.* You take one step forward. The lights go out, plunging the room into darkness.

You dash for the door, but trip over a chair in the process. You crawl frantically around the room until you find a door. But instead of the hallway you find yourself in the bathroom. Before you can back out, the door slams behind you, trapping you inside. No amount of pushing or pulling will make the door move.

You curl into a ball on the cold tile floor. Suddenly the shower and sink blast to life, spraying icy water everywhere. Water spreads onto the floor, under the door, and into the carpet. The noise bursting from the faucets drowns out your cries for help.

Hotel workers coming to find the source of the flood discover you in the morning, shivering and babbling. At the hospital, doctors can't find anything physically wrong with you. But your mind is never quite the same.

Eventually your parents place you in a private hospital. Most days you sit quietly, a model patient. You only have three strange quirks: You refuse to take showers. You never sleep on a pillow. And cell phones are forbidden.

THE END

To follow another path, turn to page 12.
To learn more about the Stanley Hotel, turn to page 101.

The silence of the lobby is unsettling. Alex said he was here. Maybe someone at the reception desk saw him.

The elegant wooden desk looks like it did when the hotel opened in 1909. No one is there, but you see a narrow wooden door behind the desk, with an ornate brass knob. A rack of old-fashioned brass room keys hangs on the wall, a reminder of the hotel's past. Above the rack are two old portraits, of a man and a woman. They're dressed in Victorian clothing and clearly were painted a long time ago.

The woman is the same one you just saw on the staircase.

Suddenly a knock comes from behind the wooden door. Then another. The doorknob begins to rattle, as though someone is trying to open it from the other side.

Your heart pounds as the knob turns and shakes. Something is trying to get out.

You've had enough of this place. You run back to your parents' room and hammer on the door until they answer. You curl into a ball on their bed and refuse to move for the rest of the night. The next morning, the storm is over and so is your family vacation. You never tell anyone what you saw, but for months your dreams are filled with the scent of roses and the sound of rattling doors.

THE END

To follow another path, turn to page 12.
To learn more about the Stanley Hotel, turn to page 101.

You head toward the Billiard Room. It was once the place where wealthy male guests gathered to socialize and play pool. Now it has a much less interesting use as a meeting room. You see Alex standing in the doorway, peering in. Slowly you creep up behind him and touch his arm. He jerks and lets out a shout of surprise. You laugh, happy that you got him for once.

"Don't do that again!" he chokes, his face white. His arms are wrapped around his middle like he's going to throw up.

"Did you ... did you see a ghost?" you ask.

He nods, his eyes wide.

You don't want to look, but Alex's eyes are begging you to confirm what he saw. You peek in the doorway. The wide meeting space is empty.

"There's nothing there," you whisper.

"Look in the mirror," Alex says.

You want to say no. You don't want to look—who knows what you might see? But you also know Alex won't be able to rest until you do. Resigned, you look into the big mirror at the far side of the room.

The mirror's reflection shows two men. They are standing beside a pool table, sticks in hand. One leans down and makes a shot. The echo of billiard balls clinking against each other floats across the room.

But when you look away, the room still appears empty.

You have the presence of mind to pull your phone out and snap a few pictures. Then you and Alex slip away from the room and find your parents.

Turn the page.

The look on both your faces is enough to send your parents into a panic. Neither of you can get the words out to tell them what you saw. Finally you pull your phone out to show them the pictures. But the pictures are just of an empty room. You and Alex exchange glances. Now no one will ever believe you. But you both know what you saw.

THE END

To follow another path, turn to page 12.
To learn more about the Stanley Hotel, turn to page 101.

The lights flicker again. Then the whole lobby seems to dim. You pull your phone out and text a couple of friends, hoping to distract yourself from the growing panic inside. By the time you get to your floor, both Alex and the uneasiness are gone.

You make your way back to your room, fiddling with your phone. As you enter the hallway to your room, a noise makes you look up.

A tall man has walked through the still-closed door of room 217. He's dressed in an elegant suit. He pauses, then looks right at you. He begins walking in your direction, a smile on his face.

The scent of tobacco fills the air as the ghost approaches. Your mind is screaming, *Run!* But you can't tear your eyes away. You can see the man's mouth move, but you can't hear a thing.

Turn the page.

You turn and run back to the staircase. At the top of the stairs, you look back over your shoulder. The man is still there, but he somehow seems less solid than he was. As you watch he fades into white fog and disappears.

Jumping down the stairs three at a time you get to the reception desk and demand another room. When you tell the clerk what room you want to move from, he nods knowingly.

"Happens all the time," he says, handing you a new key. "You're on the opposite side of the hotel now. We'll have a staff member move your bags for you. Have a nice night ... if you can."

THE END

To follow another path, turn to page 12.
To learn more about the Stanley Hotel, turn to page 101.

The ancient elevator looks like something out of an old black-and-white movie. The brass bars that line the wooden walls shake and rattle softly as the cab goes up. It seems to rise forever. You're sure you pressed the second-floor button. Or did you? You start to feel a little claustrophobic.

The elevator finally stops. The doors slide open. You're just on the third floor! *Maybe I just need to be more patient,* you think. That doesn't stop you from stepping quickly off the elevator.

You're surprised to see two children standing in the hallway—a boy and a girl. The girl laughs and runs away, her long brown curls bouncing with every step. The boy is dressed in a strange black outfit with lace at the wrists. *I can see right through him,* you think to yourself. Then you realize what that means.

Turn the page.

"Come and play with us," the boy says. He holds out his hand.

Before you can stop yourself, you find yourself putting your hand in his. Suddenly, children's laughter fills the hallway. The sound of running footsteps can be heard and felt. You can feel more than one youthful presence surround you.

Guests can choose the Ghost Adventure package, which ensures they stay in a fourth floor room. They are also given an EMF reader to monitor ghost activity.

The boy leads you down the hallway and stops in front of a room. He pulls you forward. "Come and play with us," he whispers again. The doorway seems to burst with color, pulling you in and making the walls around you spin. You feel no fear, though. When your vision returns to normal, all you want to do is play.

The hotel staff finds your body in the empty room the next day. No one knows how you got into a locked room, what happened inside, or why you never left. But today guests stepping off the elevator on the third floor are sometimes greeted by a ghost that looks like you.

THE END

To follow another path, turn to page 12.
To learn more about the Stanley Hotel, turn to page 101.

The gift shop seems like a safe choice. But you can't seem to focus on the souvenirs and T-shirts crammed into the small shop. Alex seems distracted too. Somehow you walk out with a keychain you don't remember buying. You fidget with it as the lobby lights flicker, and then go out.

There's a moment where you and Alex panic, clawing the dark air to find each other. Suddenly the room is ablaze with light. You blink against its glare. Something is wrong. The furniture in the lobby is different. The leather and wood seating areas are gone, and have been replaced by wicker. The formerly-empty lobby is crowded with people, buzzing with conversations.

In a daze you wander past men wearing suits and old-fashioned sportswear. Women in long flowing gowns gather in groups. The feathers on their ornate hats tremble in the warm breeze.

Warm? You look out the window. The raging blizzard has disappeared. You can see the majestic Rocky Mountains rising beyond the hotel's windows.

The sunlight seems to give you strength. You need more. You shuffle toward the door. Someone calls your name—Alex?—but you ignore it. You draw the door open, throwing your arms out toward the sun.

The next morning a keychain is found in the doorway of the hotel. Staff members eventually discover your body in a snowdrift a few feet outside the hotel entrance. No one can explain why you walked into a blizzard—or the smile permanently frozen onto your face.

THE END

To follow another path, turn to page 12.
To learn more about the Stanley Hotel, turn to page 101.

The Music Room sounds like a fascinating place to start. However, you find when you arrive that the room is closed. The ghost hunters pause, pressing their ears to the doors.

"People are constantly reporting that they hear piano music coming from this room," Josh explains in a low voice. "Can you hear anything?"

As much as you'd like to witness a real ghostly piano being played, you can't hear anything. The others shake their heads too, disappointed.

You're not going to let some closed doors stop you. You slowly pull the door open, and everyone creeps through. A huge black grand piano stands on a small stage near one end of the room.

You and Alex watch the ghost hunters set up cameras and microphones. Alex tells them wild stories about all the ghosts he's seen today.

You wander over to the piano and gently press a key. A quiet whisper of a note, one you can barely hear, drifts out. The piano answers you—the key depresses on its own and a single loud note blares through the room.

"Stop playing with the piano," Amy says with a jump.

"It ... I saw it move!" you say, pointing at the piano. Alex shakes his head and tries to laugh, pulling out his phone. "Say cheese, you crazy ghost," he says, snapping several pictures at once. You can see the ghost hunters rolling their eyes as they get back to work.

"W-wait," Alex says a moment later. "You have to come see this." Everyone gathers around Alex as he swipes through the images. The first five show nothing but you and the piano. When he gets to the sixth one, everyone gasps.

Turn the page.

There is the figure of a woman sitting at the piano. Her hands are resting lightly on the keys. She glows with a blue light, and you can see the piano bench through her long gown. You jump when, without warning, piano music fills the room.

Everyone looks at one another. Then you turn as one to look at the piano. A gray shadow shimmers, and then disappears. Forever after, you will swear that the ghostly music faded away with a sigh that sounded uncannily like the word, "Cheese ..."

THE END

To follow another path, turn to page 12.
To learn more about the Stanley Hotel, turn to page 101.

The tunnels under the hotel connect the hotel basement to the service entrance. Employees could use the tunnel to enter and exit the hotel unseen.

What could be more fascinating than a secret tunnel? The group makes its way to the tunnel's entrance. Staring at the dark path makes you feel claustrophobic. Mike sees your apprehension and slaps you on the back. The surprise helps you forget your fear, at least momentarily.

Turn the page.

"Don't worry, it's not a secret tunnel to unknown lands," he says. "It was built for the employees to get to and from the kitchen quickly."

The ghost hunters enter first, and you and Alex follow. You feel safe with them walking ahead of you until they switch off their flashlights. Your claustrophobic feelings return. The ghost hunters flick on their night-vision camera and its soft glow calms you a little. You can hear Alex breathing heavily behind you.

Slowly your group creeps through the tunnel. The ghost hunters pause from time to time to check their equipment or to whisper among themselves. Out of nowhere, a woman's voice cuts through the darkness: "Hello!"

You freeze. Alex gasps. The ghost hunters frantically point their cameras in the direction of the sound. The voice cries out again: "Hello!"

You see the camera light fall as the camera clatters to the ground. Then the light goes out. You turn and grab for Alex—but he's not there. Nothing happens when you reach for your phone. The battery, which was fully charged when you entered the tunnel, is dead. You drop to your knees and crawl along the ground, calling for your brother.

"Hello!" The voice is louder now, and closer. You stand up and move as fast as you can back the way you came, running your hand along the rough stone wall to use it as a guide. You didn't think you'd gone very far, but the tunnel seems to stretch on forever in this forbidding darkness. *Surely I'll find the way out soon*, you think.

Turn the page.

You hear someone running behind you. Then ragged breathing. Alex! Relief overwhelms you and you turn around to greet him.

"HELLO!"

Emergency workers find you the next morning, sitting on the tunnel floor and staring into the darkness. Alex and the ghost hunters are never found. Alone, you spend the rest of your life living inside your head. All you do now is mutter, "Hello, hello, hello ..." No one ever answers back.

THE END

To follow another path, turn to page 12.
To learn more about the Stanley Hotel, turn to page 101.

You can hear the children playing even before you get off the elevator. Mike and Amy look at each other, open-mouthed.

"We've heard of this," Amy says finally. "The ghost children. But ... we never hoped ..." She adjusts a microphone and steps out into the hallway.

The laughter dies away. Carefully you make your way down the hall. Alex stops in front of room 401 and knocks loudly on the door.

"What are you doing?" you hiss, unnerved by the ghost children's presence. "You'll wake up the people in there!"

No one answers, though. After a moment Alex pulls out his key card. "I wonder if this will work here," he says and swipes it. To everyone's astonishment the door opens with a click.

Turn the page.

Alex glances at you, grinning. He pushes the door open. The ghost hunters follow him, leaving you alone in the hallway. You take a step back. You're not going in.

Seconds later you hear several loud bangs. They sound like gunshots! Alex and the ghost hunters tumble out of the room, tripping over each other to get out.

"What happened?" you ask, helping Josh to his feet.

Room 401 was once the nannies' lounge. Perhaps tired nannies object to being intruded on by guests.

Alex slams the door and stumbles backward, falling onto the floor. He sits there, heaving for breath and shaking his head, his eyes wide with terror.

Finally Josh is calm enough to answer. "The minute we walked in there, the doors went nuts, opening and closing on their own."

"One caught me," Amy says, showing the deep red gash on her forearm.

Alex hauls himself up and grabs you by the arm. "We're holing up and not coming out until morning," he says. You don't argue. The two of you run to your room and lock the door behind you. Your ghost hunting days are over.

THE END

To follow another path, turn to page 12.
To learn more about the Stanley Hotel, turn to page 101.

EPILOGUE: THE HAUNTED HOTEL

Every list of the most haunted places in America includes the Stanley Hotel. The majestic hotel sits at the entrance to Rocky Mountain National Park in Estes, Colorado. Diehard paranormal fans from around the world flock to the hotel every year. They hope to catch a glimpse of one of the dozens of spirits that lurk in its elegant hallways and rooms.

The hotel began as the dream of one man. In 1903 Freelan Oscar "F.O." Stanley suffered from tuberculosis (known as consumption in Stanley's day.) Following his doctor's orders, Stanley and his wife, Flora, traveled to the tiny village of Estes Park in the Rocky Mountains. They hoped the fresh air would cure Stanley. It worked, and Stanley decided to stay and build an elegant hotel that would attract the finest of East Coast society.

Stanley's friends were astonished by the hotel. It had electric lighting, plumbing, telephones, and all the trappings of a high-class life—and all in the middle of the wilderness.

For years the Stanley Hotel was the mountain retreat of the rich. They were driven to the hotel in special cars known as Stanley Steamers. After Stanley died, the hotel passed through several owners. Because there was no heating system, it closed at the end of each summer season. By the 1970s, the wealthy guests were long gone and the Stanley had a reputation for being a haunted, run-down hotel.

Everything changed when writer Stephen King stayed at the hotel near the end of its season. That single night inspired King to write one of his biggest best-sellers—*The Shining*. After the book's release, people began coming to the Stanley, to experience the hauntings of the hotel.

The spirits of the Stanleys are not menacing, but there are a lot of them. The Stanleys themselves are perhaps the best-known ghosts. They have been spotted in the lobby, on the staircase, and in various rooms. Flora's ghost is usually accompanied by the scent of roses, and hotel staff believe Stanley himself has made an appearance by the smell of cherry tobacco.

Some say the Stanleys continue to oversee the hotel's operation from beyond the grave.

The hotel's fourth floor, formerly quarters of the nannies and children of the wealthy guests, is the most haunted. Fourth-floor guests report hearing children laughing, playing, and tossing a ball through the hallways.

Strange sounds, lights, shadows, voices, and spirit orbs are only a few of the paranormal sightings in the hotel.

There are hundreds of accounts of strange paranormal phenomena occurring throughout the hotel, including cold spots, otherworldly sounds, voices, and doors that open and shut on their own.

Even people who don't believe in ghosts are surprised at the thousands of photos, recordings, and personal accounts of paranormal experiences from guests. Does this mean the hotel is truly haunted? Or are all these events just the wishful thinking of a public who wants to believe? We may never know for sure.

TIMELINE

1858—Joel Estes builds his ranch on what is today Estes Park.

1903—F.O. Stanley first visits Estes Park.

1906–1907—Construction on the hotel's main building begins. An ice pond, 9-hole golf course, tennis and other outdoor courts, and ten additional buildings are also added.

June 22, 1909—The first guests arrive at the hotel.

1911—Rumors claim a gas leak caused an explosion in room 217. Maid Elizabeth Wilson is injured, yet she continues to work at the hotel until her death.

1915—Rocky Mountain National Park is created by Congress and signed off on by President Woodrow Wilson.

1926—F.O. Stanley sells the hotel. He buys it back in 1929, then sells it again.

1940—F.O. Stanley passes away.

1946—The hotel is sold.

1966—The hotel is sold again. It will be bought and sold multiple times over the next 20 years.

1974—Author Stephen King visits the hotel.

1977—King's book, *The Shining*, is published.

1977—The hotel is listed on the National Register of Historic Places.

1980—Stanley Kubrick's horror movie, *The Shining*, is released.

1984—Heat is added to the main building, allowing the hotel to be open year-round.

early 1990s—The hotel owners file for bankruptcy.

1995—The hotel is purchased for $3 million.

1997—A TV miniseries based on *The Shining* is filmed at the hotel.

2013—The Stanley Film Festival has its first year. The four-day-long festival shows classic and contemporary horror films.

2014—Pieces of drywall and carpeting matching old photos of room 217 are found in the hotel basement, reinforcing the story of the 1911 explosion.

2015—A hedge maze, based on the maze from *The Shining* movie, is opened.

2016—The property undergoes a $35 million renovation, including the addition of a wellness complex, ampitheater, film center, and more meeting space.

GLOSSARY

apprehension (ap-ri-HEN-shuhn)—the state of being worried and slightly afraid

atmosphere (AT-muh-sfeer)—the mood of a place or situation

billiard (BIL-yurd)—having to do with billiards; billiards is a game in which people use a stick, called a cue, to hit balls around a table.

claustrophobia (KLAH-struh-foe-bee-uh)—the fear of tight spaces

conspiracy (kuhn-SPEER-uh-see)—secret agreement between two or more people

décor (DAY-kor)—the furnishings and decoration of a room

EMF—a physical field created by electrically charged objects

foreboding (for-BOH-ding)—the feeling that something bad will happen

furnishings (fur-NUH-shings)—furniture and decorations, such as curtains and carpets, in an area or room

generator (JEN-uh-ray-tur)—a machine that converts mechanical energy into electricity; generators can be power sources when regular electricity goes out.

hydraulic (hye-DRAW-lik)—a system of pumps powered by fluid forced through chambers or pipes to raise and lower an elevator cab

ominous (OM-uh-nuhss)—describes something that gives the impression that something bad is going to happen

ornate (or-NAYT)—elaborately or excessively decorated

panoramic (pan-UH-ram-ik)—a very wide, sweeping view or scene

paranormal (pair-uh-NOR-muhl)—having to do with an unexplained event that has no scientific explanation

phenomenon (fe-NOM-uh-non)—something very unusual or remarkable

psychic (SYE-kik)—a person who claims to sense, see, or hear things that others do not; some psychics say they can sense and communicate with ghosts.

skeptic (SKEP-tik)—a person who questions things that other people believe in

spirit orb (SPIHR-it ORB)—balls of light believed to contain peoples' spirits or souls

tuberculosis (tu-BUR-kyoo-low-sis)—a disease caused by bacteria that causes fever, weight loss, and coughing; left untreated, tuberculosis can lead to death.

vortex (VOHR-tex)—a whirling mass of light connected to ghostly activity

OTHER PATHS TO EXPLORE

In this book you've seen how terrifying being alone in a haunted place can be. But haunted places can mean different things to different people. Seeing an experience from many points of view is an important part of understanding it.

Here are a few ideas for other haunted points of view to explore:

- A hotel needs a staff to run. But what happens if the staff is afraid of the hotel? Imagine you work at the Stanley Hotel. Would you be afraid, or would you bravely go into every room and tunnel?

- Over the years, the Stanley Hotel has had many owners. If you owned the Stanley Hotel, how would you run it? Would you play up its haunted past, or try to present it as a regular hotel?

- The hotel offers many opportunities to experience its resident ghosts. What kind of haunted tour would you go on? Would you rely on ghost hunting tools, or let the ghosts surprise you?

READ MORE

Owings, Lisa. *Ghosts in Hotels*. Minneapolis: Bellweather Media, Inc., 2017.

Peterson, Megan Cooley. *Haunted Hotels Around the World*. North Mankato, Minn.: Capstone Press, 2017.

Summers, Alex. *Haunted Hotels*. Vero Beach, Fla.: Rourke Educational Media, 2016.

INTERNET SITES

Use FactHound to find Internet sites related to this book. All of the sites on FactHound have been researched by our staff.

Here's all you do:
Visit *www.facthound.com*
Type in this code: 9781515736509

INDEX